NIGHT COLLAGE

for Ted,
beloved travelling companion

Annie Deppe

NIGHT COLLAGE

Night Collage

is published in 2021 by
Arlen House
42 Grange Abbey Road
Baldoyle, Dublin 13, Ireland
Phone: 00 353 86 8360236
arlenhouse@gmail.com
www.arlenhouse.ie

978–1–85132–237–4, *paperback*

Distributed internationally by
Syracuse University Press
621 Skytop Road, Suite 110
Syracuse, NY 13244–5290
Phone: 315–443–5534
Fax: 315–443–5545
supress@syr.edu
syracuseuniversitypress.syr.edu

Typesetting by Arlen House

cover image:
'Alma'
by Caitlin Deppe
is reproduced courtesy of the artist
Photograph of painting by Ben Lewando

CONTENTS

Blessed are they who remember
that what they now have they once longed for.

Anonymous lines found by Jean Valentine *on a bulletin board, which she quotes in her poem* 'The River at Wolf'

The most beautiful sea hasn't been crossed yet.

Nâzim Hikmet, *from* 'What I Haven't Told You Yet'

What is the source of our first suffering? It lies in the fact that we hesitated to speak. It was born in the moments when we accumulated silent things within us.

Gaston Bachelard, *from* Water and Dreams

Night Collage

In Flew Chaos

It had been snowing for hours
when the pounding began.
Thinking it one of my teenage children

finally home on a Friday night but without a key,
I left my book to open the door
and into the kitchen's warmth flew chaos.

A young woman, shaking, in a thin dress,
snow-covered hair and no shoes,
arms flailing at something I could not see,

screaming, and then the sudden silence
as she yanked me down to a crouch.
So he won't see us.

What brings such disorder to mind now?
On this morning's walk, we found
the storm had rearranged the strand.

A foot or more of sand
was washed away exposing
jagged rock crops we hadn't known were there.

On hands and knees, the girl and I
watched from the hall window
a slow dark sedan slide by,

snow falling in its headlights.
Her fingernails biting my arm, the quick
shhh – he will kill me if he sees us.

My husband was oblivious, doing something
we called *sleeping fast* before driving
unploughed roads across two states to reach his job.

When I was a girl, a woman came waving
a silver revolver at another back door.
Only glass between.

My mother who liked to read mysteries
late into the night let this stranger in
and sat chatting with her

at the kitchen table while I listened
from the next room. I kept trying to picture
where the gun was.

By the time my sons and daughter got home,
the ambulance was gone. On the table, by his bowl
and morning cup, a note for my husband.

And my mother and her *woman with the gat*
as it was handed down in family stories,
what was she thinking? What was I?

I always knew I would do anything
to keep my family safe,
but where had my good sense flown?

Her pupils were dilated.
As they lifted the stretcher
all I could do was give her hand a squeeze

and tell her it would be all right. *Damn it.*
Even as her body surrendered to the straps,
I couldn't help being glad to see her go,

but something wild had visited,
something had knocked at the storm door
and been let in.

GRANDFATHER FIRE

The Iroquois Theatre, Chicago, 30 December 1903

This could be a poem about doors
that only open inwards. Ten-foot-high
piles of bodies crushed against them.
A woman, who wasn't my grandmother,
and her son who was never an uncle.

The glorious woodwork, the long velvet curtains.
The laws now requiring
doors to open out. Birdie, Taylor:
part of my mother's prehistory
she tried to bury. And her father Jack Dryden

(I never knew they called you Jack)
who made and lost a fortune or three,
a family or two. Jack
who after the crash, ended alcoholic
in a New York City room

designed like a boat, shipshape –
everything pared to the bone
like a survival craft, though
you didn't survive. Fire. Water.
The dirt of potter's field.

How could you bear to breathe
the air of that saloon turned morgue?
In its charred chaos
only a custom-engraved Christmas watch.
Only a pair of gold fluted earrings.

Meditation on the Gift of Feet

Our neighbour waves as he carries his bucket of scraps
down to the cove. Twice each day,
a cloud of herring gulls heralds his arrival.
Tonight we're enjoying our supper outdoors
as insatiable seabirds and sleek black crows rise
from the water. Our talk drifts back

to the Christmas Eve dinner
when a fifteen-year-old son did not come home
and how, after the rest of the family
put out the tree lights, I climbed
into his bed to wait. How did we all survive
those teenage years? In my mind, only accident

or worse could keep a son away that night.
And if it turned out he was dead, what then?
The one clear thought I remember
– before he arrived home safe, if unapologetic –
was I would put on my shoes and walk my grief
till I could come up for air:
the Cumberlands, the Blue Ridge, the Smoky Mountains.

That litany of Appalachian ranges echoes again
as the mountains of Mayo create tonight's horizon.
And I recall how years earlier, we heard the news
about Three Mile Island at a table in Kentucky.
Separated from my parents in New England,
I swore I would take off and walk
to find them there – a thousand miles distance –
if the crippled nuclear power plant
permanently shut down the grid.

Now, our family is spread across two continents.
Water is rising. Both the Arctic and the Amazon

are going up in flames. The state of lungs
in what might be the first weeks of a pandemic.
If life as we know it ceases to be, how does a mother
mother when an ocean lies between?

Salt Meadow

I'm sweeping and thinking of my father
when you call me over

to watch a dog careening
through early summer

in the field between our house
and the sea. First here,

the head's quick flight
above the grasses, its fur russet

as the foxes of my childhood,
then gone. The meadow itself

soon to be mown,
the smaller and smaller circles

of the haying coming near again.
My father's words rimmed with age:

I am getting edged off.
He didn't mean it kindly.

Grace again – for it is Grace,
our neighbours' dog –

ears hanging in the air
like a bird's copper wings

then falling from sight.
The grasses of the field,

like promises of abundance. Or like
the return of all these swallows.

My father's words mixing
with my worries

over just how much will be enough
to see us through.

The Wind Around the Gunwales

Back then I was the sort of girl
who was sure someone would die
if the phone rang while I climbed

the stairs, so I raced.
Nights I would lie in bed
hiding in my mind from murderers.

A minister's family. I learned
to smile through everything
but never to talk.

By twelve that smile was adrift
in red. I almost broke that smile
leaning hard into its scaffolding.

This repetition of the smile here –
is it too much for you? Well, I had my act
down so well until at fifteen

I danced with a man
who whispered in my ear
You're a fake

and all that protection simply
tumbled. And where
can a person go from there?

It took decades
before I understood
how it's possible to be too nice.

I suppose one could say
that smile became a boat with
ribs broken beneath the skin.

Or, for those who could read it right,
the wind sorrowing around the gunwale.
But to that girl, it was a refuge

carved high into a mountainside.
Almost inaccessible. A place she imagined
she could shelter in.

NESTLING, GREEN

And so, hardly noticing,
we've entered the lengthening
white nights of Connemara summer
and though it's late

we walk out through the long lingering
reflected in the bay.
Beyond Inishturk
the slow sun seems to take its time

as we follow the water's edge
to the sea wall and the field
where the smell of grass
cropped by two ponies and their foals

fills the air. We breathe it
all in. How to slow
life to a saunter,
so we can take in the changes

all around, the nestling green
on the reedy cliff,
the waving yellow flags of June.
Even the spiky plant

whose name
I can't recall has sent forth
its tall, speared furl.
More than once, love, you've said

This is paradise, and if paradise
keeps changing, you might be right.
A pair of oystercatchers
dib and whistle, then lift

to circle the low flat tides of light.
Each sharp note a fractal
of this shared life. Each green change
containing the whole.

We are not One and the Same

It has taken almost two decades to realise
we meant different things by selling
our house and crossing the sea.

What I didn't understand
was it might be almost forever
before we would reconstruct those birch-lined walls:

paper bark curling above the snowy fields,
one child holding his own children now,
and our hair grown white

as winter morning grass. The sea rolls in, the sea clatters out.
My heart carried like the cloud
of dunlins swooping in perfect symmetry.

Or torn like this ...

Blue No Where

We've come this far
from the Kingdom of Noise.

Left behind, a life so stressed we raced
to reach the post office before its close,

found ourselves empty-handed, letters
home on the kitchen table.

Eight miles out, windy headland
of sea and shifting sky, Cape Clear,

no place else we want to be.
You write. I hum. Blue No Where.

Reading the Weather

Since arriving on this island
we've taken in each day's forecast
with our morning coffee
as we listen to the maritime report.
This hilly rock is a ship at sea
in the North Atlantic.
Last night, an orange moon
above the soft cluck of shore birds.
Ever fewer boats
out on Roaring Water Bay.

The end of September
and I woke this morning to find
for the first time in months
my knees are without pain.
Like the deep silence
of a power cut, they feel
a glorious nothing.
Eleanor's suggestion of slow stretching
is the miracle balm
so this morning the shipping news
of my inner weather
has turned a fleeting blue.

Trumpet

Once there were two sets of stairs:
the front ones curving and formal,
while the backstairs rose steep
as a canyon wall. As a girl,
I used to fly from their heights.

Strange to be transported back to childhood
as I climb a footbridge to what remains
of Civita di Bagnoregio, a small hill town
like an island in the sky, surrounded
by spectacular nothingness.

Looking up at the projected journey
I was terrified,
but now, safely within the walls,
there's a rush of energy, a feeling
of never being more inside my body

exploring a tangle
of two-thousand-year-old lanes
that all end at the brink.
The stone church's relics of Bonaventure,
a wooden manger in an Etruscan cave,

bruschetta with garlic toasted over coals,
and a framed photo of a man on a horse
barrelling down
an earlier incarnation of the footbridge,
his face lit by something wild.

My brother's room was at the top
of our backstairs. I am haunted still
by the sounds of weeping
beyond his door. But other times
there were the golden notes of a trumpet,

creating a space in his bedroom
for something so much larger.
I hear him now playing Bach
in this Italian town where every century or so
another house or lane lets go.

What Carlo Might Have Said

There once was a man or perhaps
once there was a monk
who lived in the Piedmont hills.
One day he left his house, or monastery,
walked out of the village
until he came to the edge
of the field with three white rocks,
where he knelt down and didn't get up again
for thirty years, at least I think
that's what Carlo said,
but I know little Italian
and he has not much more English.
The seasons cartwheeled, the stars
performed their silent dance.
Over time, a pair of finches
nested in the rags of his hood
mistaking him for a tree. And still
he knelt on. This reminded me
of Saint Kevin, though
Carlo insisted, no, no.

And then the morning of the first day
of the thirty-first year he rose
and without hurry made his way
home again. As far as I could understand,
the tale doesn't say whether
his wife waited for him
or whether the order built
or tore down walls. There
seems no moral to the story.
Just a man went out to a field
knelt and stayed and watched
and studied until he began
to take in the world. And then
went home.

OUTSIDE HOWTH

As the train passes what I call
the Japanese house, clouds darken the bay

and I pull my thin coat
tighter around my shoulders, the same coat

I was wearing when, arriving home from work,
I thought it too late to return my mother's call.

She was dead by morning.
I once read the story of a woman

travelling through the mountains of Hokkaido
and how she lost the child she carried within.

A village doctor told her
our lives flow into us, so each of us starts out

something of a water child, not yet solid
or fully in this world until the age of seven.

And how we begin to leave this life again
and return to those waters at the age of sixty.

A gradual process, this turning of the tides,
this slipping away. So short a time solid.

So short a time fully in this world.

Homage to James Joyce

Tonight as our taxi enters Kreuzberg
under the flare of a summer storm,
the first hushed chords of Brahms rise
from the radio just as our driver
incongruously begins to croon *hoppy birthday*
to you. I wonder who he sings this to?
On unlit corners, men gather after a hot day
of fasting: above, Ramadan's bright unfolding.

It's been fifteen years since I sang *A German Requiem*
after my mother's death. Now it mixes
with a birthday song and the sky's
flashing crescendo. *The ineluctable modality*
of the audible. The taxi pulls up
to Falckensteinstraße 20 and its tall scarred doors.

While Thinking on My Youngest Son

my study fills with autumn
as the brown ducks resurface
in the Tiergarten pond

the clock is made of yellow
little capsules of acorn bursts
like the clatter of time

in a borrowed book in Berlin
I've just found a photograph
of someone who looks a lot like you

in it a man cradles a baby and cat
his apparent contentment
warming that saved afternoon

the fall of hair around your eyes
the melancholic yearnings
the way the heart holds hope

what pleasure the birch
beneath my window
brings with each new year

Kreuzberg: The Intimacy of Strangers

Friday morning, seven o'clock,
and I'm drowsing in bed reconsidering
a visit to the fruit and vegetable man
whose day it is to come from the country
and set up his wares on a corner
three blocks from here

– all those tempting fruits bearing German names
but I'm limited to what I can carry.
And that problem of touch.
His unwelcome assumption of intimacy.

Shouts draw me to the window:
a pair of men, alive with curses,
anger-dance their way
down cobbled Falckensteinstraße.

Elegant graffiti explodes nightly
on the red door opposite ours

but on the bench beneath the linden tree
two Turkish women chat together
unperturbed. Between them
an orange bag overflows with onions.

Breakfast of the Birds
after Gabriele Münter

This is in Murnau.
  This is after
the darkness
fell. Yet today, it seems

as simple
  as a table placed
before the window
set with two

  white plates.
One with fresh rolls.
One empty but ready to
receive what comes next.

It's as though
  it all comes down
to a conversation
between a woman

  and those
early-morning birds
that glide
  to their own table

with the expectation
of what will be
  provided.
They descend and rise

and descend again
  from snow-sprung
branches. How does one paint
this morning's songs?

While Passing Through the Living Room During a Pandemic

I catch a quick glimpse on the television
of a chorus performing Fauré's *Requiem*
and find myself consumed with envy.
I need to sing like that again.
The filling with voice. Such joy
to come together to transcend
boundaries and become,
somehow, something larger.

Though then, concert over,
the inevitable letdown. The programmes
left scattered on auditorium seats.
Our music folders all turned in. Snow
falling beyond the great oak doors.
This life, this life.

X-Berg

we're back in Berlin
walking down our streets
back in night-town Kreuzberg
walking graffitied streets

reach Miss Tilly's Dance Club
the lights have all gone out
the lights have all gone out
the lights have all gone

I sent her a letter
but she never replied
wrote a letter in the airwaves
never heard a word

back on this funky *Straße*
Tilly's music's gone
Tilly's music's gone
Tilly's music's long gone

Song of the Wheel in the Key of Green

Somehow between those round overflowing bowls
of salad greens and spicy rocket
and my quick *oh!*
when one of the candles lit for lunch goes out,
I'm recalling how close death came, years ago,
when on the third night, after that terrible fall,

I sat propped by pillows late and alone
in the spare bedroom, sick and damaged-to-the-edge.
Sleepless with pain. A glowing green wheel
rolled in, its energy flowing
to a place catty-cornered opposite

and came to hover beneath the ceiling.
Not the feathered thing I'd hoped for,
more like a wagon wheel of startling
spring-green spokes with an essence

deeply feminine like a spiralling back
through family or kin I somehow knew,
though when had we ever met?
Come with us ...
For too many years a low

vibrating note of darkness
lined my soul, a grinding music
melancholic and ever-present;
now I was given the opportunity to lift
and go. It's not that the invitation

wasn't attractive – it was –
but forced to choose, I found myself saying *No,*
though I will need your help to stay.
Let me be absolutely clear, this was not

a dream. A dozen years now, and we leave
our curtains wide to Connemara.

Evenings, from the lane, neighbours sometimes see us
reading to each other and it feels as if
they're peering not into our home
but into our hearts. This shared life: open late
like a library or a night museum. Winged. Abiding.

Squall

She told me she would cut me
    off-centre to spare the belly button.
She told me my scar would fade
    to moonlight, but it never did.

Father Felix told me
    he would hear my confession –
Father Felix told me
    he could sing me lullabies from Nigeria.

You said I was a boat
    your hand would try to anchor.
Then something wintry
    assaulted the windows

and the foot of my bed
    rose and slipped its mooring.
I told myself make for safe harbour.
    Make for the sound of singing.

On Not Seeing Bernini's Angels

We have lived in this cottage by the sea
for seven years but now it's up for sale.

A fresh coat of paint, red trim
of windows. The sally tree

where the wrens once sang, removed.
Still the swallows soar through rain.

I am having trouble
getting an answer from my sister

about how her medical tests went.
Sorting through my desk this morning

I came upon a slip of paper:
We become orphans together,

our parents gone.
In the city of life and death,

fifteen years back, they slid me
into the round opening of a machine

that hummed. They told me
not to move. Afterwards,

no one would look me in the eye,
and I was left alone in a wheelchair

waiting for an orderly,
everyone's paths parting around me

like water. I understood
the news must be bad.

Two days after surgery my sister
sat at my side

while my husband and daughter
left to see Bernini's work

at the Fogg Museum. Their favourite part:
the five-hundred-year-old,

pinched, terracotta sketches of angels.
One with its drapery blown open,

furled back over a leg as though
by a gust of wind. In the show's catalogue

– I know this can't be true but
we're dealing here with angels

– X-rays appear to reveal
surprising hollows of light

within those seraphim
like the invisible tattoos of last rites

I will carry till I die.
We arrived home from the hospital

to find the power out, snow falling
on an owl on the barn's steep roof,

and my body radically changed.
None of that mattered.

I know someday we must
all move on from these glorious homes

but for a while longer we get to linger.
I hope my sister's news will be good.

107 Water Street

in memory of James Merrill

She paints alone at night in the glassed-in room
built at star level, and when she looks up
she's squinting at a space beyond the window

as though into another room suspended in air
above the street, a place where briefly
you seem to be gazing back at her.

Night after night, she's half-expecting
to find you seated at the milk glass table,
white gauze curtains lifting in the breeze,

but it's in that thin space beyond
the glass she finally sees your face.
Something in her thinks a soul

could get lost in such a room,
or find itself, daily, in the making.
Decades now, since Maya Deren burned

the sugar heart into the floorboards
just inside your door. Even as it fades
from sight, the conversation continues.

FROM CAPE CLEAR ISLAND TO COUNTY GALWAY

Abandon a walking trip
eight miles out to sea to find
one of the few places left on earth

you can wander dark lanes at night
and not hear even the faintest sound
traceable to humans. How many

decisions are shaped like this?
Birch trees and sycamores
guided us for more than a decade

until we came to that Irish island
and walked beneath
her silent canopy. Then north

along the mainland's coast to where
curlews call – those trills – and something
of Wittgenstein comes back:

I can only think clearly in the dark,
and in Connemara I have found one of the last
pools of darkness in Europe.

Yesterday NASA released
a photograph of Ireland at night
with bright constellations of towns and cities

but at the end of this peninsula
not far from Wittgenstein's Killary,
our dark headland keeps its silence.

NOVEMBER, RENVYLE

Lingering in bed
beneath the new blue quilt:
coffee and porridge
and grey sweeping waves.
Cloud shadows on Mweelrea
across the bay.
A warm proximity, shared view
but everything changing
in lag time. Long seconds
before the ponies you commented on
will wander into my sight.
Then hay carried in a sack.
Legs touching, everything close
but angled so differently.
The breaking-blue window of sky
travelling your way, inch by inch.

The Singing House

That autumn in Tully Cross,
the months slipping from green to tan,
the presence of George Herbert

keeping me company
beside Derryherbert's rising hill,
there were times when

I sat at the table alone,
no one else at home,
and an indistinct melody line

would lift from somewhere
within the house
then blossom into multipart

harmonies of humming
or vibrating string-song, and I
wondered whether this drifting gift

sometimes from the side and at others
from behind my skull
was part star-song or brainstorm

or messages from beyond
or appliance
or entirely imagined. My husband

never heard it. We didn't live there long.
Several years later,
a few townlands away,

I read about an operation
on a young man with a tumour in his skull,
who loves music – whose life *is* music –

and how his doctor mapped
his brain through MRI, then prodded
to try and find where his

gift dwells. The doctor's goal:
to spare that sacred place within.
Midway through the operation,

still awake, tethered
to machines, brain exposed,
he was handed his saxophone, golden

and glowing, and told to blow.
It's as though our souls
work from the inside out

to form a chord
of rhythms and vibrations
to manifest a place of harmony.

I'd like to think the surgeon went home
and heard a night chorus
from his refrigerator

or wherever such melodies come from.
Music rising within four walls, as outside
the wind backs in from the west.

What Now Goes by the Name of Home

I had forgotten that this is the bargain set from the start:
we come in alone and go back the same.

Conception by thunderstorm
then the long welcome into a month's

cave of loneliness.
Steeple, convent, that house in Missouri where

a flustered woman entered with her glinting gun.
There've been close to thirty and still counting.

The Tin House with her singing clattering roof,
the marriage house with its night of a hundred tornadoes.

Green skies in the morning. The colour blue
not yet conceived and the contents of dreams

spirited into an earthenware bowl.
And now it's Castle Cottage, named

for the pirate queen's tower next door.
Ancient battles lingering in the castle's cove,

through sideways rain, above the sea.
Everything permeable.

What troubles me most
is not the growing list of pencilled addresses

but the feeling of family
somehow thinning. Despite the scatter

of jewels across the last porch roof,
are we not still tucked in together, somehow,

wherever we are? But the worry
that the house called family might be emptying

is enough to wake me up most nights.
I thought it would be forever. Its own Jerusalem.

Elegy for Madam Bridget

Outside the Supermac's in Galway,
a young garda cast a shadow
over Madam Bridget.
Her cloudy blue eyes

studied the people
in Eyre Square as he
wrote out a fine. The cardboard
sign against her stool. The cigarette

in yellowed fingers. Four sugars
and a bit of milk. How many times
did we watch her turn the tarot cards?

She was the real thing, you know,
she could tell you
anything you wanted about love.

TRAÜMGOLD

for Joan and Kate Newmann

I'm telling Theo about the moss green alcove,
fern banks rising like choruses, feathery fiddleheads

edged with gold as though thousands of notes
were released from the embroidered bag

our poet friends left behind.
They will need it soon but it brings such joy

and from the moss green alcove I hear a kind of hum,
an undercurrent, a heart's beat behind my own.

It is like my mother is dreaming the rise
and fall of my speech and echoing back

the laughter. My dead mother just beyond,
following with pleasure the joy of life.

I call out to her, and Theo wakes me. Gives me a kiss
to take my nightmare away.

'*Why* would I want you to take her away?'
And just like that, I am lost on this continent

like throwing a party for too many people
who are unable to come (I can't stop weeping).

Get out the map to find our way back
to the great green canyon of ferns.

Open the window to let in the night:
the wind, the salt and the traffic of the sea.

Waking to Find Ted Gone

Ted's note this morning
    speaks of the early fog
and how it was like drinking
    coffee in North Beach.
He's out there walking now.
    What I want to tell him about

is the night birds,
    how they streamed past
on their way to the ruined tower
    with their whooshing
wings of emptiness.
    He said

the Golden Gate Bridge
    might be sailing through that fog
somewhere. I say the birds
    separated
round our house like water
    parting for a river rock.

Otherwise Known as Grace

Strolling up through early summer
through ragged-robin and buttercups
to the ruined Church

of the Seven Daughters
I reach the grave of our friends' young son.
Actors, they inscribed his stone

with Shakespeare: *We are such stuff*
As dreams are made on, and our little life
Is rounded with a sleep.

My children live in worlds
so different from mine,
and though I've never lost one

I'm struck by how the older I get
the less certain of anything
I become. Whatever happened

to wisdom with age?
Doors close one after another
even as the light off sea

opens and shuts.
Everything, it seems,
keeps changing.

Sometimes, I know that love is hard
and you must work
to keep connected.

Sometimes, whole days go by
when I know nothing
except sea salt and blustering wind.

Staying with Mrs West

Stooping through the little door
of her chicken coop – the one
with the gun nailed above the sill –
we entered the gloom
of cluck and murmur.
Earlier she'd told me out by the clothesline
– white sleeves slapping above my head –
Anne, you'll need to learn to work hard
because those Russians are going to take our land,
but here we were in a dusky,
comforting country where time slowed,
then seemed to almost stop
like all those years of the chair placed
beside her husband's bed. Sometimes
when he was having a bad time of it
she'd let me sit at the top of the stairs
and listen as she played the mandolin for hours.
Strange now to realise he'd been back from the war
for forty years and yet his lungs
– those ravaged battlegrounds –
would still outlast her playing by a decade.
But for that moment, there we were
in the murky hen house
and I still had no idea what would happen next
after she selected one hen
and carried it under her arm to the waiting yard.

The Little Rehearsals

After the fall
backwards and the rock-
hard blow to the head
it was not exactly
dark (there was
that star-filled cliché)

but I was rendered
absolutely still,

and then for weeks
there was the loss of
balance like walking
drunk down
stairs until that day
in Arches

where you cupped
my head with your hands
and steadied me
beneath Balanced Rock.

That summer, back home
in Ireland, there was an inner
slippage, no, knots

that burst and spread
like gorse fire
along the IT band,

crippling
my leg until I could no longer
cross the room.

From our window I watched
couples. I watched families.
I watched our neighbour
lean into the wind

to reach his cows. All
these rehearsals. Sometimes
in the long weeks until
my footing was restored, I watched
the tourists walk the cliff road
and found myself weeping

for the gift of
locomotion as easy
as breathing.

Meditation Across Two Continents

It's not that I want to take the years
and peel them back
like the paper layers of a wasp's nest
in winter. Or reattach the strips
of birch bark lost in banks of snow.
But there are nights when the thrush
begins to sing in Connemara
that I realise I've begun to forget
the bird songs of my childhood.

The storage unit which by now
could have bought a small house
would empty. The green goblets,
retrieved from the far dark corner,
allowed again to brim.

Though it would mean no more mornings
with the white mare led along the sea
past a row of vanished houses.
Or sweet storms sweeping the mountains.
But how does one pour the whiskey
and the laughter back into the bottle
and tell our friends – and ourselves – it's time
to go home again?

And of course it's not that simple.
It's as though someone
took the photos lining my desk's edge
and shuffled them until no one
and nothing quite fits
together. In the old way.

It's dawn and that thrush
keeps holding forth.

Can’t I celebrate its song
and still stay loyal
to the music of birds
whose names I’ve almost forgotten?

Either way, a shoebox
packed like family waits,
or in my darkest nights, is released.

On the Night Before First Grade Begins

I am lifted and placed on the wall three storeys below
my father's hospital window and told to *turn* and *turn*
so he can see my new school clothes:
smocked plaid dress and shiny red shoes.

Peering up, I can't see him. It is as if
he is hidden in the heights.
In our Christmas photos that year, we are all smiles
except my father – his mouth has settled to a grimace.

But that first Wednesday morning of September,
as I wait for the bus, the line of maples before our house
bursts with colour as though everything

– even a benevolent presence
watching from above – was still possible.
Those guardian leaves. Red hope of new shoes.

And When the Red Wine of Minervois

turned out to be white,
my guard let down, the word slipped out,
'I need to bring the *worsh* in from the line.'
How many years has it been?
I must have been all of seven when I realised
only my mother, brought up in Bryn Mawr,
ever spoke of *worsh*cloths.

Soon I could say wash with the best of them.
Wash the dishes, do the wash,
my father reminding me always
to wash between my legs.
The washcloth strategically floating
over him during our shared baths.

There are so many things I've never
gotten to tell you, Mother,
and my shame over your accent
was undeniably the least.

I will bring in the *worsh* from the line tonight,
I will make up my marriage bed,
I will rejoice in the sun calves
frolicking the cliff road above the sea,
I will try and find the right words to say
what has never been said.

Windwalk: The Fifth of January

In the brief hour between winter storms,
we pause to watch a raft of gulls
float upon the shallow bay, then rise in rings
against the snowy mountain beyond.
Too easy to project and make them
into metaphors. My father, dead.
Now, yours. And all the rest.
Turning, we pass the local school bus driver
checking out the green coach
waiting by his house.
His round face lifts.
They go back tomorrow,
but in these gales – he shakes his head –
it's like a roller coaster.

What makes up a child's life?
For six years, as Mr Kallgren's yellow bus
travelled back roads, I was the last child
let off each day. If he were here,
if he were somehow part of that spiralling host,
I would thank him
for comforting Linda
whose father had just arrived home
from prison. Even at ten,
I knew beyond my years
why he was put there.
Mr Kallgren opening the bus door.
Linda slowly stepping down.
That terrible power.
How does a child go on
holding the fate of her family?

Night Collage Seven

I could sit *shiva* for Sky, if I lived near
her loved ones. Instead I pull up a stool
and listen to the night, seek out
the lights on Clare Island until low clouds
move in and seem to snuff them,

and I think how in Cold War Berlin
they planned to turn down the air
in the fallout shelters
so no one had the oxygen to rebel.
Closer to home, our neighbour is hurrying

along the sea lane through the dark.
What is needed in the barn this late?
Imagine. Not enough oxygen.
But that's the problem.
We can't imagine.

People have returned
to the house up the hill
and every window is ablaze.
Together, they make a city,
a miniature Jerusalem.

After the winter storm departed
we found the gunwale of a wooden boat
washed up in our garden, and from somewhere,
decades ago, my mother's voice reciting: *Where
did you come from, baby dear?*

*Out of the everywhere
into the here.*
I miss my friend who once
lived in the heart of Venice.
Salve, Sky. Salve.

Who knows where this all ends up.
All those watery stars.
If I knew how, I'd pull up this island
like a low chair and listen for you.
Or rebuild that boat and row.

Houseboat

1

The slender green slip of a boat
has appeared again,
this time unnaturally at home
on North Atlantic waters. Early morning's
thin light shimmers against her keel.

Every few years she shows herself:
The Studio Boat, The Wren.
Tea Boat in Little Venice.
This time an invitation onto open waters,
like a portent. But what if this appearance

floats a different sort of shift?
Even a spirit level is useless
in all this movement, so a new
measure is needed. Why is it
something in me begins at the end?

What elsewhere might be
a coot or swan
knocking at night on the boat's side,
here is a transatlantic tern,
a curious pecking at sleek dark wood.

Like the tap of a pocket watch.
Or the shaking
after giving birth
as a body simultaneously
releases and takes on change.

2

Once again, we will be wanderers.

Before daybreak she floats like a dream
in this liminal space,

that impossibility of a houseboat
gliding over ocean waters.
On her bow's curve

I can just make out three letters, *Grá,*
or maybe it's the start of Gráinne?

We push out from the cove, look back

at our home from the sea
as if lingering in that dream state.

The wind comes round
and we find ourselves
turned towards the west.

Precious string of islands.
The never ceasing

slip-sound of water.

3

Jot down the image of the boat.
Then lock the red door, drive past the pirate queen's
ruined castle, pause at the car park
where once a tour bus of French sightseers
set up folding tables and created their own dream.

White linens, champagne in sunlit flutes,
as a Connemara pony looked on.
Once again, we are wanderers. We must trust
we will be given what we need to sustain us.
Copper roof with sweet tattoo of rain.

The lapping. The table. Everything changing
but journeying with us.
Even a pony (*Hello, Beauty).*
A boat like a house whose name
might well be Gratitude.

ACKNOWLEDGEMENTS

Thanks to the editors of *Sojourners Magazine, The Stinging Fly, The Hartford Courant, Honest Ulsterman, The SHOp, On the Seawall, Dodging the Rain, Drawn to the Light, Atticus Review* and the anthology *Washing Windows? Irish Women Write Poetry* (Arlen House, 2017), where some of these poems have appeared.

About the Author

Annie Deppe was born in Hartford, Connecticut, and is a dual citizen of Ireland and the United States. She is the author of *Sitting in the Sky* (2003) and *Wren Cantata* (2009), both published by Summer Palace Press.

Literary magazines on both sides of the Atlantic have published her poems, including *Poetry Ireland Review, The Stinging Fly, Honest Ulsterman, Sojourners, Sou'wester, The Recorder,* and *The SHOp.*

Her work has appeared in many anthologies, including *The Forward Book of Poetry 2004; Fermata: Poets and Writers Respond to Music; If Bees are Few: A Hive of Bee Poems; Dogs Singing; Washing Windows? Irish Women Write Poetry;* and *Landing Places: Immigrant Poets in Ireland.*

She was awarded a BA in English from Earlham College, an MA in Educational Psychology from the University of Connecticut and an MA in Creative Writing from Lancaster University.

She has received grants from the Arts Council/An Chomhairle Ealaíon and from the Arts Council of Northern Ireland. She was selected by Poetry Ireland for their Introductions Reading Series.

She works for Stonecoast in Ireland (part of the University of Southern Maine's Stonecoast MFA Programme). She lives on the west coast of Ireland.